DEBATING THE ISSUES

The Electoral College

Sue Bradford Edwards

MEDIA ENHANCED BOOKS AV² BY WEIGL ADDED VALUE • AUDIO VISUAL

www.av2books.com

Published by AV^2 by Weigl
350 5th Avenue, 59th Floor
New York, NY 10118
Website: www.av2books.com

Library of Congress Cataloging-in-Publication Data

Names: Edwards, Sue Bradford, author.
Title: The electoral college / Sue Bradford Edwards.
Description: New York, NY : AV2 by Weigl, [2020] | Series: Debating the issues | Audience: Grades 7 to 8. | Includes index.
Identifiers: LCCN 2018051724 (print) | LCCN 2018055117 (ebook) | ISBN 9781489696182 (Multi User ebook) | ISBN 9781489696199 (Single User ebook) | ISBN 9781489696168 (hardcover : alk. paper) | ISBN 9781489696175 (softcover : alk. paper)
Subjects: LCSH: Electoral college--United States--Juvenile literature. | Presidents--United States--Election--Juvenile literature.
Classification: LCC JK529 (ebook) | LCC JK529 .E39 2019 (print) | DDC 324.6/3--dc23
LC record available at https://lccn.loc.gov/2018051724

Printed in the United States of America in Brainerd, Minnesota
1 2 3 4 5 6 7 8 9 0 22 21 20 19 18

122018
112318

First published by North Star in 2018

Project Coordinator: Ryan Smith   Designer: Ana María Vidal

Every reasonable effort has been made to trace ownership and to obtain permission to reprint copyright material. The publishers would be pleased to have any errors or omissions brought to their attention so that they may be corrected in subsequent printings.
Weigl acknowledges Getty Images, iStock, Shutterstock, and Alamy as its primary image suppliers for this title.

The Electoral College

Contents

Understanding the Electoral College 4

Timeline 7

PROS

The Electoral College Balances Power 8

The Electoral College Prevents Regional Control 14

The Electoral College Creates a Clear Winner 20

CONS

Electors Might Not Vote as Expected 26

The Electoral College Gives Some Voters More Power 32

The Electoral College Does Not Represent the People 38

Pros and Cons Summary 43

The Electoral College Map 44

Quiz 46

Key Words/Index 47

Log on to www.av2books.com 48

A person must be 18 years old and a U.S. citizen in order to vote in a federal election.

Understanding the Electoral College

Every four years, people throughout the United States vote in the presidential election. This process is known as the popular vote. Technically, people are not voting for the president. Instead, their votes determine which **electors** will represent their state.

There are 538 electors in all. Each state has a certain number of electors. To become president, a **candidate** must receive 270 electoral votes. In most cases, the candidate who wins a state's popular vote earns all of that state's electoral votes. However, Maine and Nebraska are different. In these states, two electoral votes go to the candidate who wins the state's popular vote. The other electoral votes go to the person who won the popular vote in each **congressional district**.

Electors take part in a second vote. This happens one month after the presidential election. Votes from each state's electors are recorded on a Certificate of Vote. Certificates from all 50 states and Washington, D.C., are counted in a joint session of Congress. This is when the president is officially selected.

The term Electoral College refers to this entire process. This process has been used to choose the president for many years. However, some people believe it is unfair. They suggest using a different method instead.

UPDATING NUMBERS

Throughout history, the U.S. population has grown. The number of states has increased as well. As the country grew, the number of electoral votes also changed. In 1789, George Washington received 69 electoral votes, the highest number possible. By 1888, a candidate needed 201 votes to win. Today, a candidate must win 270 votes.

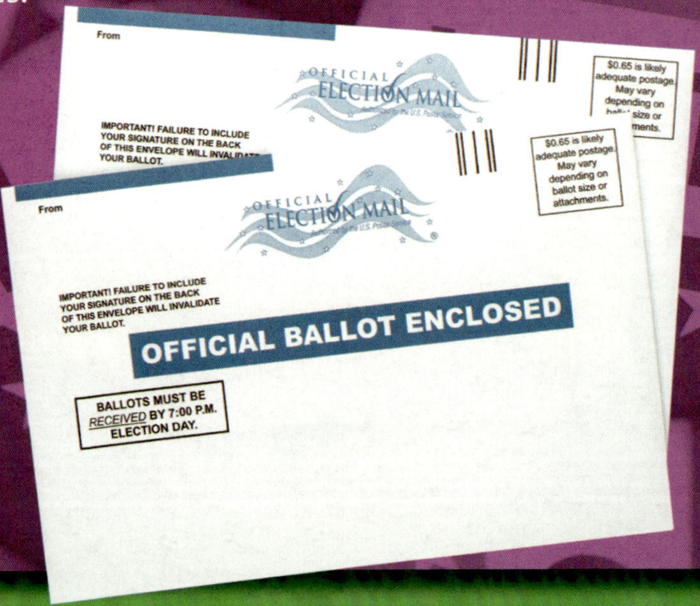

Timeline

1787 The Constitutional Convention amends and approves the Electoral College system proposed by the Committee of Eleven on Postponed Matters.

1804 The Twelfth Amendment is ratified. Voters now fill out separate **ballots** for who they want to be president and vice president.

1824 John Quincy Adams is the first president to lose the popular vote. He is awarded the presidency by the House of Representatives.

1961 The Twenty-third Amendment is passed. Residents of the District of Columbia are given representation in the Electoral College.

2016 President Donald Trump is elected after winning the electoral vote, 304 to 227, over Hillary Clinton. This is the fifth time a president is elected without winning the popular vote.

2020 In December, the number of electoral votes allocated to each state will be adjusted to reflect its population as recorded in the 2020 Census.

PRO

Arizona's 2010 population of 6.4 million granted the state 11 electoral votes in the 2016 presidential election.

The Electoral College Balances Power

In the United States, the federal government is the central power. State governments are the regional powers. The Electoral College helps make sure these two powers stay balanced. This balance of power is an important part of the U.S. Constitution. **Delegates** from the states met in 1787 to create this document. They worked to create a strong central government, but they wanted states to have power, too. There were delegates who thought members of Congress should elect the president. Others wanted state governors or state legislatures to choose. Some even called for democratic elections by the people. Delegates created the Electoral College as a compromise. In this system, electors from each state vote for president and vice president.

The Constitutional Convention ended with 12 states signing the U.S. Constitution.

Some delegates thought all states should have the same number of electors. However, larger states often make up a bigger part of the U.S. economy. Plus, more people live in these states. If all states had the same number of electors, small states would have an unfair advantage.

Instead, the number of electors is based on how many members of Congress each state has. States get one elector for each member of the Senate and one elector for each member of the House of Representatives. Every state has two senators.

ELECTORS IN EACH STATE (2016–2020)

The number of Electoral College representatives for each state will be updated after the 2020 census.

States with higher populations have more representatives. Therefore, these states get more electoral votes. Those states with smaller populations have fewer electoral votes. For example, Iowa's population is small. The state has only four representatives. Iowa gets one electoral vote for each of these representatives and two more for its senators. Therefore, Iowa has a total of six electors. In contrast, many more people live in the state of New York. This state has 27 representatives. That means New York has a total of 29 electors. Giving larger states more votes ensures they have an appropriate amount of influence.

In 2016, Hillary Clinton held more than 270 speeches and rallies during the election cycle.

The Electoral College also helps balance the power of the federal government with the power of the states. To win 270 electoral votes, a candidate must win votes in many states. Each candidate must learn what voters in these states want or need. For instance, Hillary Clinton was the Democratic candidate in the 2016 presidential election. Clinton gave a speech in Cleveland, Ohio. She promised to bring 376,000 jobs to the state. Candidates must address various concerns of people from around the country.

PRO

New York City had more than 4 million eligible voters during the 2016 presidential election.

The Electoral College Prevents Regional Control

The Electoral College helps rural states, such as Wyoming, have more influence on election results.

The Electoral College also prevents some states from having too much control. If presidential elections were based on the popular vote, states with larger populations would have more influence on the results. These states would get far more votes. For instance, California has a population of more than 39 million. In contrast, Wyoming's population is only 590,000. California has nearly 67 times as many people as Wyoming. Therefore, California would have much more influence in a direct election.

Furthermore, candidates in a direct election would likely focus on large cities. They might ignore states where people are more spread out. The Electoral College helps motivate candidates to **campaign** in rural states. In 2016, Maine hosted three campaign events. Nebraska had two. Mississippi held one. Without the Electoral College, rural states would be unlikely to attract as much attention.

The Electoral College gives small states the power to make their opinions heard. One example of this is the 1876 election. Rutherford B. Hayes ran against Samuel J. Tilden. Voters in small states supported Hayes. These states were too small to have much of an impact on the popular vote. Tilden received 264,000 more popular votes than Hayes, but Hayes received one more electoral vote. He won the election.

Rutherford B. Hayes chose to only serve one term as president.

Small states become especially important in close elections. In 2000, experts predicted a very close race. Every electoral vote mattered. Democratic candidate Al Gore and Republican candidate George W. Bush worked hard to win support. Even small states were important. New Hampshire, for example, has only four electoral votes. The state's population was approximately 1.2 million in 2000, while the U.S. population was more than 281 million. New Hampshire's residents would have little influence in a direct election, but both candidates knew it was important to win New Hampshire's electoral votes.

President George W. Bush won the 2000 and 2004 presidential elections.

In addition, the Electoral College prevents one region of the country from controlling the election. For example, Grover Cleveland won large majorities in six southern states in 1888. He won a total of 18 southern states, giving him the most overall votes, but Cleveland lost in the rest of the country. As a result, his opponent Benjamin Harrison received more electoral votes and won the election. Supporters of the Electoral College say it worked as designed in this election. It prevented a candidate with only regional support from winning.

Did You Know?

In 1961, the Twenty-third Amendment gave Washington, D.C., three electors. Until then, the residents of this city could not vote in presidential elections.

President Benjamin Harrison lost the popular vote by more than 95,000 votes.

PRO

In the event of a tie, the Constitution requires Congress to select the president and vice president.

The Electoral College Creates a Clear Winner

In the 2016 election, presidential candidate Jill Stein demanded a recount of the votes cast in Michigan.

The Electoral College makes it easy to determine who wins an election. In some races, no candidate wins a majority of the popular vote. This happened during the 2000 election. That year, Democratic candidate Al Gore received 50.9 million votes. Republican candidate George W. Bush received 50.4 million. Green Party candidate Ralph Nader received 2.9 million. No one received more than 50 percent of the vote. Bush won 271 electoral votes, which was enough to win the election, but the popular vote was very close in Florida. Some people did not think Bush should win that state's electoral votes. Florida's Supreme Court ordered a recount of the ballots. As the votes were counted, Bush's lead in the state shrank. The recount dragged on until December 12. Then the U.S. Supreme Court called for it to end. Bush was given Florida's electoral votes and was declared the winner.

Without the Electoral College, a close election might require more extensive recounts. Instead of counting the votes in only one state, people might have to recount popular votes from throughout the entire nation. This process could take much longer.

The Electoral College also helps resolve elections in which no candidate wins more than half of the electoral votes. In this situation, Congress determines who will become president and vice president. The House of Representatives selects the president. Representatives vote on the three candidates who got the most electoral votes. The Senate chooses the vice president from the two candidates with the most electoral votes.

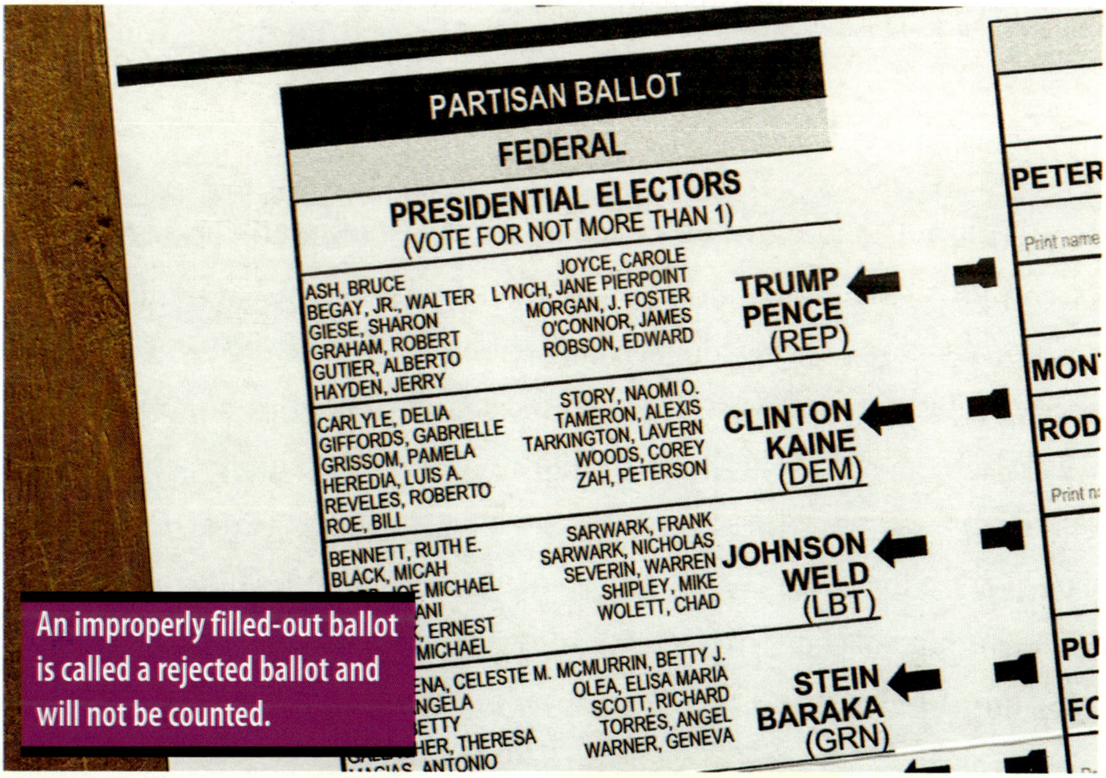

An improperly filled-out ballot is called a rejected ballot and will not be counted.

In the 1824 election, President John Quincy Adams lost the popular vote by almost 45,000 votes.

This situation is more likely in elections with three or more **viable** candidates. For instance, no candidate won the majority in the 1824 election. Andrew Jackson had the most popular votes and the most electoral votes, but John Quincy Adams was a close second. Henry Clay and William Crawford came in third and fourth. Even though Jackson had gotten the most votes, the House of Representatives chose Adams to be president.

In addition, the Electoral College ensures a swift transfer of power. Electors almost always vote for their party's candidate. So, **statisticians** can often predict who will win the election before the electors vote in December. Statisticians look at popular vote totals in each state. As the votes come in, they can guess which candidate will win that state's electoral votes. Sometimes, they can even tell who will win before voting is finished. This gives government workers more time to prepare for the new **administration**.

Exit polls, along with precinct and county vote totals, allow statisticians to project who is going to win an election before all the votes are counted.

CON

Despite only Donald Trump and Hillary Clinton winning electoral votes in the 2016, seven people received votes from the Electoral College.

Electors Might Not Vote As Expected

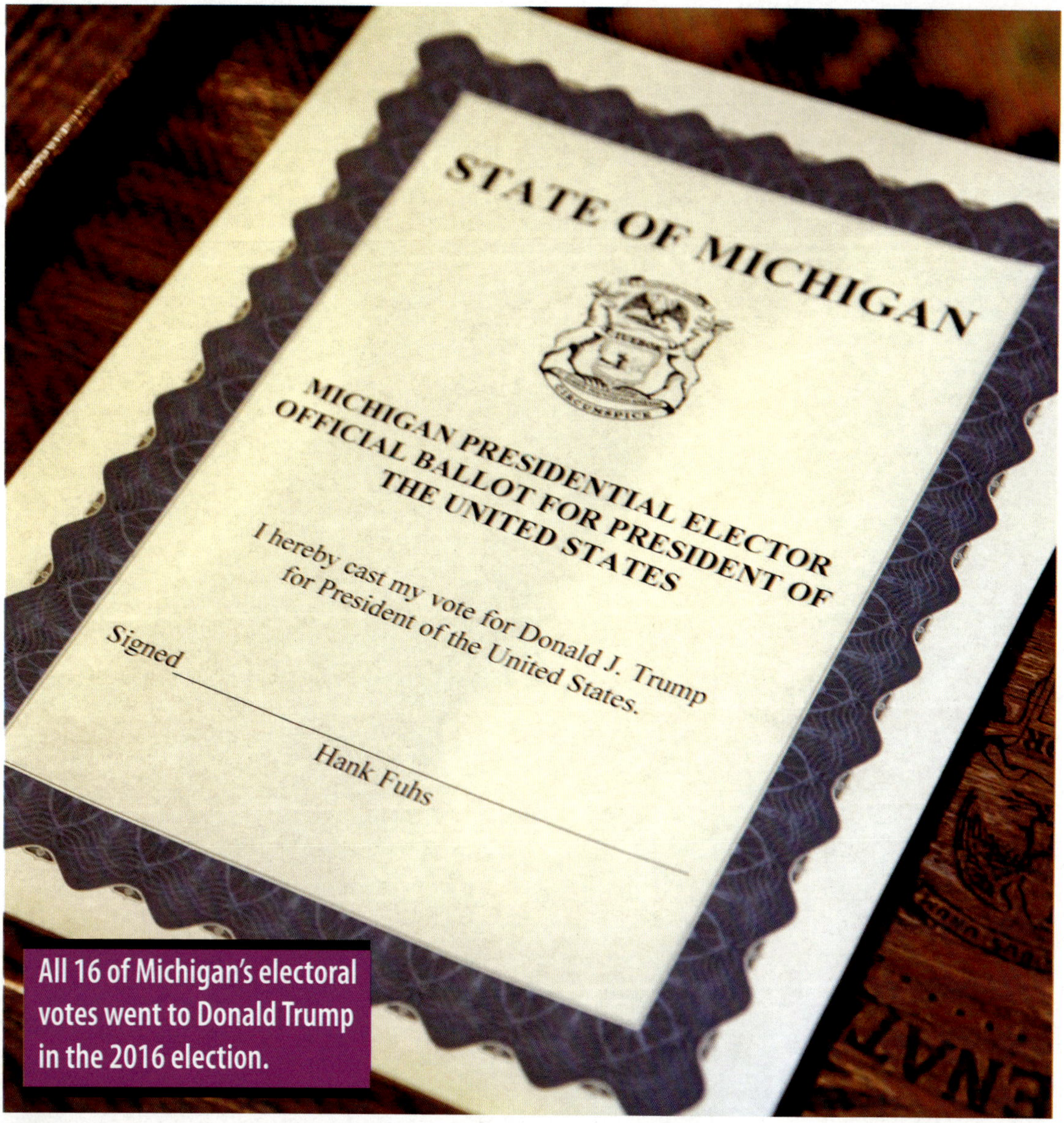

All 16 of Michigan's electoral votes went to Donald Trump in the 2016 election.

If the Republican candidate wins the popular vote in a state, the state's Republican electors get to vote. These electors are expected to vote for the Republican candidate. If the Democratic candidate takes a state, the Democratic electors vote. They are expected to vote for the Democratic candidate. People often act as if these choices are certain. But electors do not always vote for their party's candidate.

An elector who does not vote for the party's candidate is called a faithless elector. States try to discourage faithless electors. Certain states make their electors swear an oath. Other states require faithless electors to pay a fine. But many states do not have consequences. Some states have consequences that are not very severe. Electors sometimes ignore them.

For example, Hillary Clinton won the popular vote in Hawai'i in 2016. The state's Democratic electors got to vote. In Hawai'i, a law requires electors to vote for the candidate who wins the popular vote.

After electors cast their ballots in their home states, the ballots are sent to Washington D.C. to be counted in front of Congress.

However, one elector, David Mulinix, voted for Bernie Sanders instead. By voting for Sanders, Mulinix was protesting the Electoral College. He did not think it served people well. The Hawai'i law does not discuss a penalty for faithless electors, so Mulinix was not punished. In Minnesota, electors must swear to vote for their party's candidate. Muhammad Abdurrahman broke his pledge in 2016. Clinton won the popular vote in Minnesota. But Abdurrahman voted for Sanders instead. Minnesota's secretary of state rejected the vote. He replaced Abdurrahman with an alternate elector, who voted for Clinton.

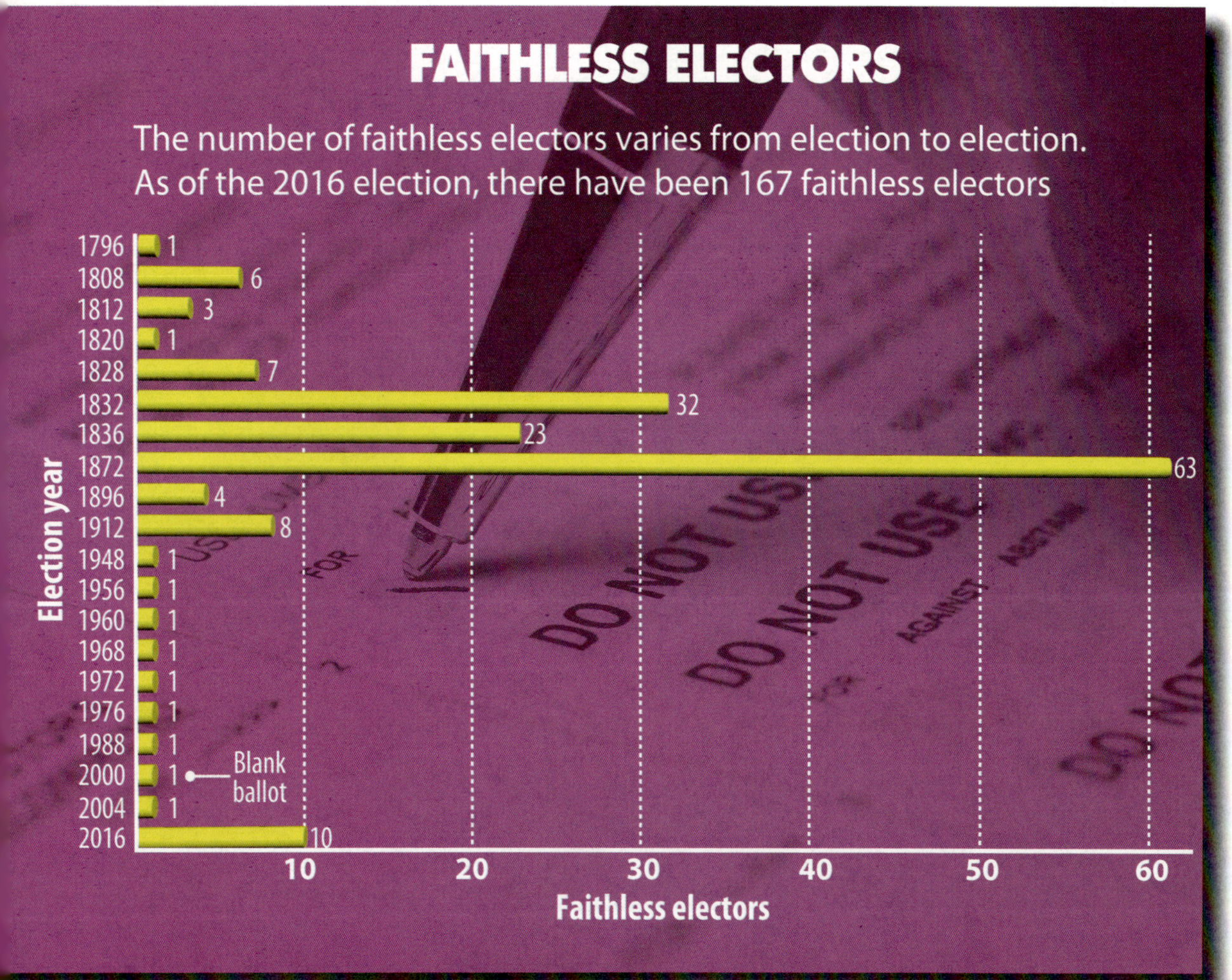

In 2016, four Washington electors also chose not to vote for Clinton. A Washington law fines faithless electors. The electors had to pay $1,000. This was the first time in the law's 30-year history that an elector was fined.

Before the 2016 electoral vote, some protesters called for electors to ignore the results of their state's popular vote.

Several elections throughout U.S. history have included faithless electors. So far, faithless electors have never swayed the results of an election. In each case, the same candidate would have won if all electors had voted as expected. Still, critics of the electoral process worry that one day that may change. If many electors do not vote as expected, it could be difficult to predict which candidate will win the election.

CON

Presidential candidates tend to focus on undecided states near the end of their campaigns.

The Electoral College Gives Some Voters More Power

Due to the Electoral College, some peoples' votes influence the election's results more than others. Specifically, people in large states have less of an influence than people in small states. For example, 39.25 million people live in California. This state has 55 electoral votes. That means California has one electoral vote for every 714,000 people. Only 590,000 people live in Wyoming. But the state has three electoral votes. As a result, Wyoming has one electoral vote for every 195,000 people. The vote of one person from Wyoming will affect the election results more than the vote of a person from California. Critics of the Electoral College say that this is not fair. Presidential candidates know that votes in some states are more influential. They will pay more attention to these voters.

During his campaign to be the Republican nominee for president, Rand Paul made stops in Nevada, an important undecided state in the 2016 election.

The Electoral College also affects how candidates campaign. States such as California, Texas, New York, and Illinois have large populations. Therefore, they should also have a significant influence in the election. But voters in these states typically vote for one political party. For example, Texas's electoral votes went to the Republican candidate in all ten elections from 1980 to 2016. California's votes went to the Democratic candidate in the seven elections from 1992 to 2016. Candidates often assume they will win the electoral votes of states that tend to support their political party. They do not campaign as much in these states.

Instead, candidates focus on states where no political party has a clear majority. These are known as battleground states. If a candidate can change the minds of only a few hundred voters, he or she may be able to win the state's electoral votes. So, candidates work harder to address these voters' concerns. For example, Pennsylvania and Ohio are both battleground states. In 2016, both Democratic candidate Hillary Clinton and Republican candidate Donald Trump visited these two states more than any other state. However, neither candidate campaigned in Tennessee or Kentucky.

BATTLEGROUND STATES

Pennsylvania has 20 electoral votes. Ohio has 18. Candidates work hard to win votes in these battleground states. In 2008, Democratic candidate Barack Obama won the states' electoral votes. He won both states again in 2012. However, Republican candidate Donald Trump won the electoral votes from both Ohio and Pennsylvania in the 2016 election.

Most battleground states have medium or large populations. Candidates also tend to overlook states with the smallest populations. These states have only three or four electoral votes. Unless an election is very close, candidates tend to focus on states with more electoral votes. Opponents of the Electoral College believe this is not fair to the American people.

Despite the presidential election occurring in November, the presidency is not officially won until after the electoral ballots are counted on January 6.

CON

Voters may feel like their voices have not been heard when the popular vote does not align with the electoral vote.

The Electoral College Does Not Represent the People

In some cases, a candidate wins the popular vote but loses in the Electoral College. In the 2000 election, Al Gore led the popular vote by more than 500,000 votes. However, George W. Bush won the electoral vote. Even though more people had voted for Gore, Bush became president.

Before Bush won Florida's votes, Gore was leading by 20 electoral votes.

Hillary Clinton won the popular vote by an even larger **margin** in 2016. In fact, she had the third-highest total of any candidate in history. Clinton received nearly 3 million more votes than Donald Trump. But she received only 227 electoral votes. Trump won the election with 304 electoral votes. Once again, the person who became president was not the person most voters supported.

Only eight percent of African American voters voted for Donald Trump in the 2016 election.

Critics of the electoral system worry that it also fails to represent minority voters. Statistics showed that Bush led among white male voters in the 2000 election. He lagged among voters who were African American or Latino. Female voters, urban voters, and people with below-average incomes did not typically vote for Bush either. Despite his narrow band of supporters, Bush won the electoral vote and became president.

Similarly, Clinton won more votes from African Americans, Asians, and Latin Americans than Trump did in 2016. But she still lost the election. Critics say her loss proves that the Electoral College works against minorities. The election results did not reflect their opinions.

In addition, minority voters often live in cities. Cities tend to grow faster than rural areas. However, the number of electors is only updated every 10 years. As a result, minority voters are more likely to live in areas that are not represented well. States with large cities may be at a disadvantage, too.

Did You Know?

The last serious attempt to eliminate the Electoral College was in 1970. A bill was passed by the House of Representatives, but it failed in the Senate.

In fact, the electoral system can make people think that their votes do not matter. This can discourage people from voting. Only 58 percent of eligible voters took part in the 2016 presidential election. In a direct election, states with high voter **turnout** would have more votes in the total. This would give them a stronger influence on the election. More people might be encouraged to vote.

This is not the case with the Electoral College. No matter how many voters turn out, the state has a set number of electoral votes. Unless these problems are addressed, critics of the Electoral College believe the presidential elections will not represent the views of the people.

Pros and Cons Summary

PROS

- The Electoral College motivates the federal government to consider the interests of the states.
- The Electoral College gives states proportional power.
- The Electoral College prevents one region of the country from controlling the election.
- The Electoral College helps to ensure rural areas are not ignored.
- The Electoral College creates a clear winner.
- The Electoral College makes it easy to predict election results and transition between administrations.

CONS

- Some electors do not vote for their party's candidates.
- The Electoral College makes some people's votes worth more than others.
- The Electoral College causes politicians to focus on battleground states and ignore voters in other areas.
- The candidate who becomes president may not be the candidate that most people supported.
- The Electoral College does not adequately represent minority voters.
- The Electoral College can make people feel that their votes do not count and discourage them from voting.

The Electoral College Map

The Electoral College is a system, rather than a place. Electoral voters cast their votes in the capitol building of their state. While most states cast all of their electoral votes to align with the state's popular vote, some states choose to represent themselves in the Electoral College in different ways.

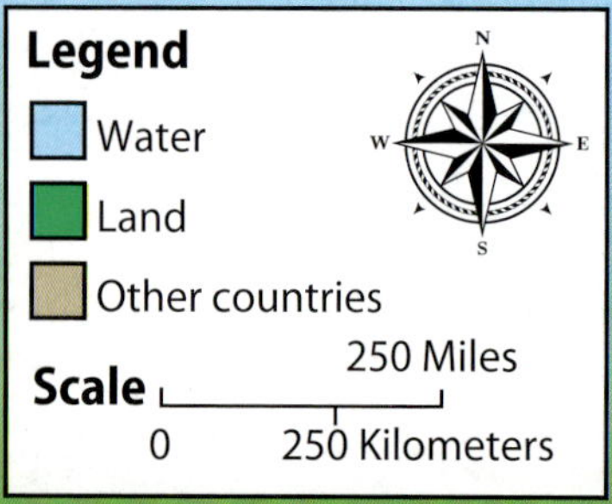

Nebraska State Capitol, Nebraska
Nebraska awards three of its five electoral votes to the candidate that wins in each of its three congressional districts. The other two votes go to the candidate who wins the statewide popular vote.

Connecticut State Capitol, Connecticut

On May 24, 2018, Connecticut became the twelfth jurisdiction to join the National Popular Vote Interstate Compact. If enacted, participating states would vote for the candidate that won the national popular vote, rather than the most votes in their respective states.

Maine State House, Maine

Maine awards two of its four electoral votes to the candidate that wins in each of its two congressional districts. The other two votes go to the candidate who wins the statewide popular vote.

The Capitol Building, Washington, D.C.

On every January 6 following an election, the Senate and the House of Representatives meet to conduct the official tally of the electoral votes. The incumbent vice president oversees the tally.

Quiz

1 Which two states split their electoral votes between the winner of the state and the winner of the national popular vote?

2 How many presidents have been elected without winning the popular vote?

3 How many electoral votes are needed to win the presidential election?

4 What determines how many electors a state gets?

5 How many faithless electors were there in the 2016 presidential election?

6 Who determines which candidate will become president if no one wins more than half of the electoral votes?

7 How many days did the 2016 presidential candidates spend campaigning in battleground states?

8 By how many votes did Hillary Clinton win the popular vote in the 2016 presidential election?

ANSWERS **1.** Maine and Nebraska **2.** Five **3.** 270 **4.** The number of Members of Congress a state has **5.** 10 **6.** Congress **7.** Clinton spent 81, Trump spent 118 **8.** Nearly 3 million votes

Key Words

administration: the group of people who work in the government's executive branch under a specific president

ballots: machines or slips of paper that are used to record a person's vote

campaign: when political candidates do work, such as traveling or speaking, to convince people to vote for them

candidate: a person running for a political position or office

congressional district: an area that elects a member of the House of Representatives

delegates: people who are selected to vote, act, or attend meetings on behalf of other people

electors: people who are chosen to represent their state and vote for the president

margin: the gap between the winner and the loser in an election

statisticians: people who analyze information having to do with numbers

turnout: the number of people who vote in a single election

viable: likely able to succeed

Index

battleground states 36, 37, 43, 46
Bush, George W. 18, 22, 40, 41

campaign 16, 17, 32, 34, 35, 36, 37
Certificate of Vote 6
Clinton, Hillary 7, 12, 13, 26, 29, 30, 31, 36, 37, 41, 46

Democratic Party 10, 13, 18, 22, 28, 29, 35, 36

faithless electors 29, 30, 31, 46

Gore, Al 18, 22, 40

House of Representatives 7, 11, 23, 24, 42, 45

popular vote 5, 7, 16, 17, 19, 22, 23, 24, 28, 29, 30, 31, 38, 40, 41, 44, 45, 46

Republican Party 18, 22, 28, 34, 35, 36

Senate 11, 23, 42, 45

Trump, Donald 7, 13, 25, 26, 28, 36, 37, 41, 46

Log on to www.av2books.com

AV² by Weigl brings you media enhanced books that support active learning. Go to www.av2books.com, and enter the special code found on page 2 of this book. You will gain access to enriched and enhanced content that supplements and complements this book. Content includes video, audio, weblinks, quizzes, a slide show, and activities.

AV² Online Navigation

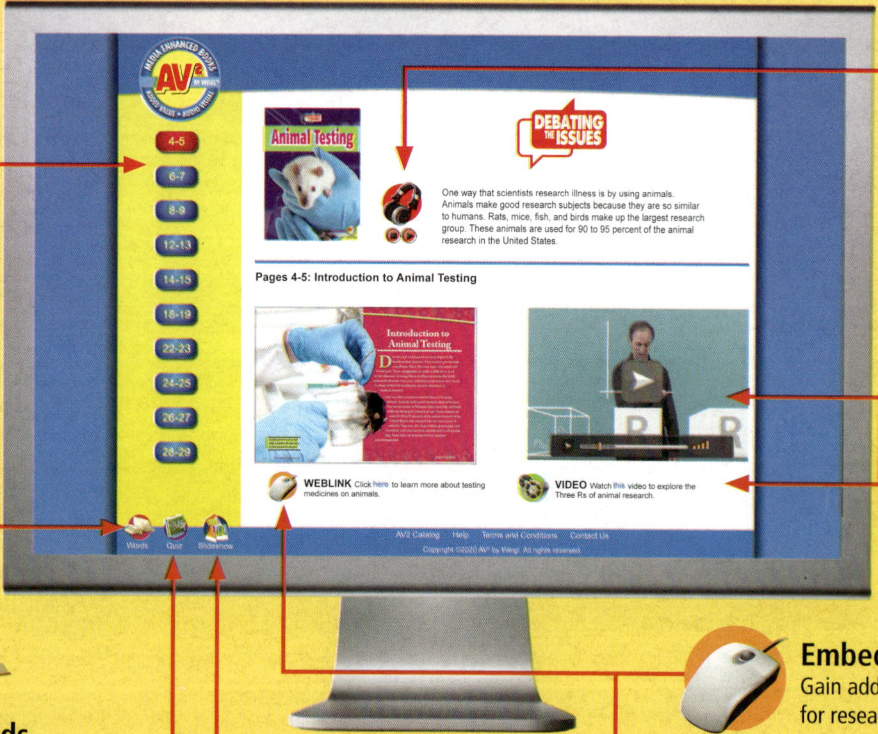

Book Pages
AV² pages directly correspond to pages in the book.

Audio
Listen to sections of the book read aloud

Video
Watch informative video clips.

Embedded Weblinks
Gain additional information for research.

Key Words
Study vocabulary, and complete a matching word activity.

Try This!
Complete activities and hands-on experiments.

Quizzes
Test your knowledge.

Slide Show
View images and captions, and prepare a presentation.

AV² was built to bridge the gap between print and digital. We encourage you to tell us what you like and what you want to see in the future.

Sign up to be an AV² Ambassador at www.av2books.com/ambassador.

Due to the dynamic nature of the Internet, some of the URLs and activities provided as part of AV² by Weigl may have changed or ceased to exist. AV² by Weigl accepts no responsibility for any such changes. All media enhanced books are regularly monitored to update addresses and sites in a timely manner. Contact AV² by Weigl at 1-866-649-3445 or av2books@weigl.com with any questions, comments, or feedback.